THE UNITED STATES GOVERNMENT

VICE PRESIDENT

NorwoodHouse Press

FRANCIE DOLAN

Cataloging-in-Publication Data

Names: Dolan, Francie.
Title: Vice president / Francie Dolan.
Description: Buffalo, NY : Norwood House Press, 2027. | Series: The United States government | Includes glossary and index.
Identifiers: ISBN 9781978581647 (pbk.) | ISBN 9781978581654 (library bound) | ISBN 9781978581661 (ebook)
Subjects: LCSH: Vice-Presidents--United States--Juvenile literature.
Classification: LCC JK609.5 D65 2027 | DDC 352.2390973--dc23

Published in 2027 by
Norwood House Press
2544 Clinton Street
Buffalo, NY 14224

Designer: Rhea Magaro
Editor: Tricia Hoffman

Photo credits: Cover, p. 1 Sergey Kamshylin/Shutterstock.com; cover, p. 1 Joseph Sohm/Shutterstock.com; p. 5 VectorMine/Shutterstock.com; p. 6 DNB STOCK/Shutterstock.com; p. 7 Phil Mistry/Shutterstock.com; p. 8 hyotographics/Shutterstock.com; pp. 9, 11, 16, 17 Wikipedia; p. 12 Chuck Kennedy; p. 13 Lawrence Jackson/The White House; p. 14 Mehmet Eser/Shutterstock.com; p. 15 mark reinstein/Shutterstock.com; p. 18 Joshua Sukoff/Shutterstock.com; p. 21 Philip Yabut/Shutterstock.com;

Printed in the United States of America

Some of the images in this book illustrate individuals who are models. The depictions do not imply actual situations or events.

CPSIA compliance information: Batch #CSNHP27: For further information contact Norwood House Press at 1-800-237-9932.

TABLE OF CONTENTS

THE UNITED STATES GOVERNMENT

The United States **Constitution** tells how the nation's government is organized. There are three parts, or branches. They are the **executive** branch, legislative branch, and judicial branch.

The vice president is part of the executive branch.

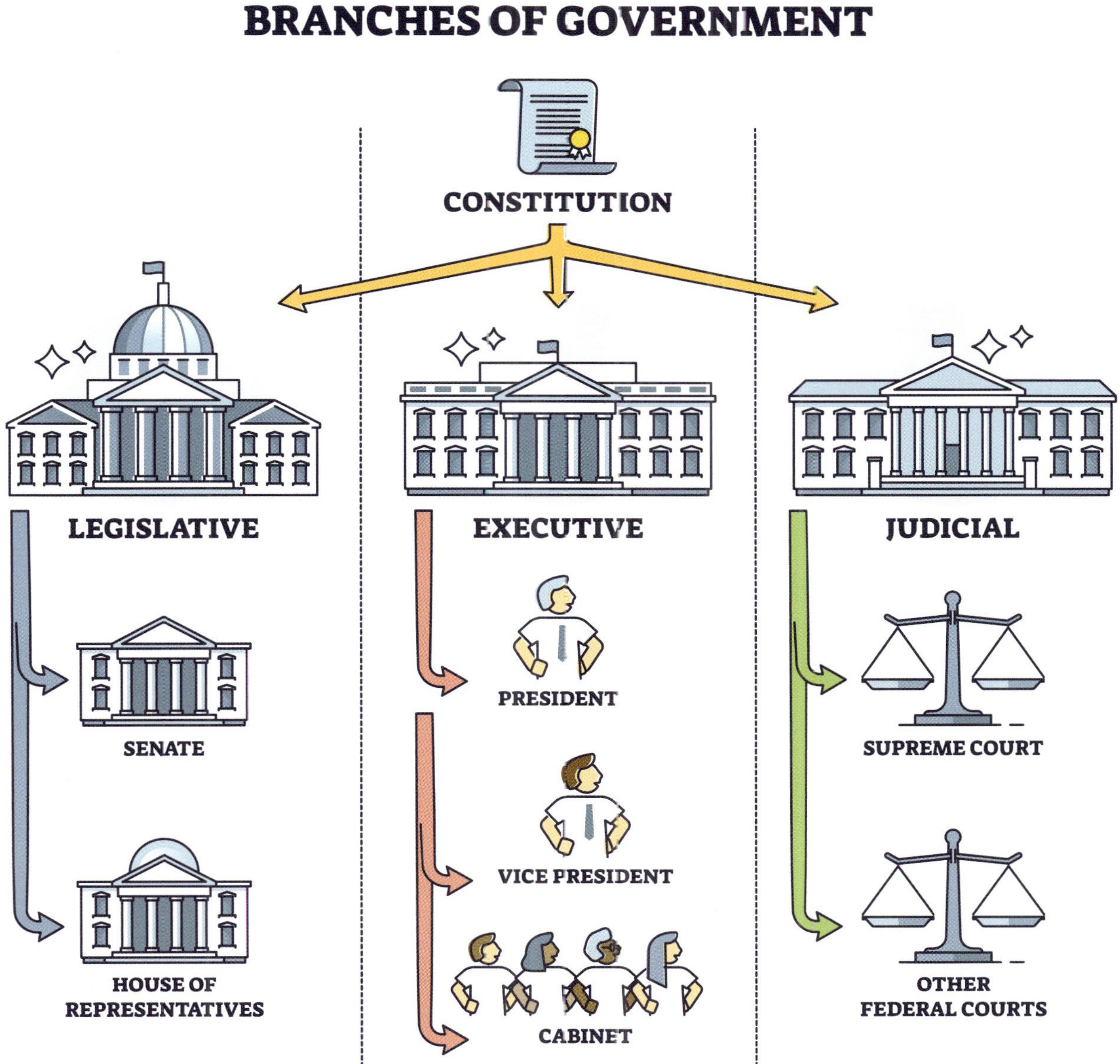
BRANCHES OF GOVERNMENT
CONSTITUTION
LEGISLATIVE
EXECUTIVE
JUDICIAL
SENATE
HOUSE OF REPRESENTATIVES
PRESIDENT
VICE PRESIDENT
CABINET
SUPREME COURT
OTHER FEDERAL COURTS

SECOND IN COMMAND

Every four years, the American people elect a president. They actually elect a pair of people—a president and the president's **running mate**, or vice president.

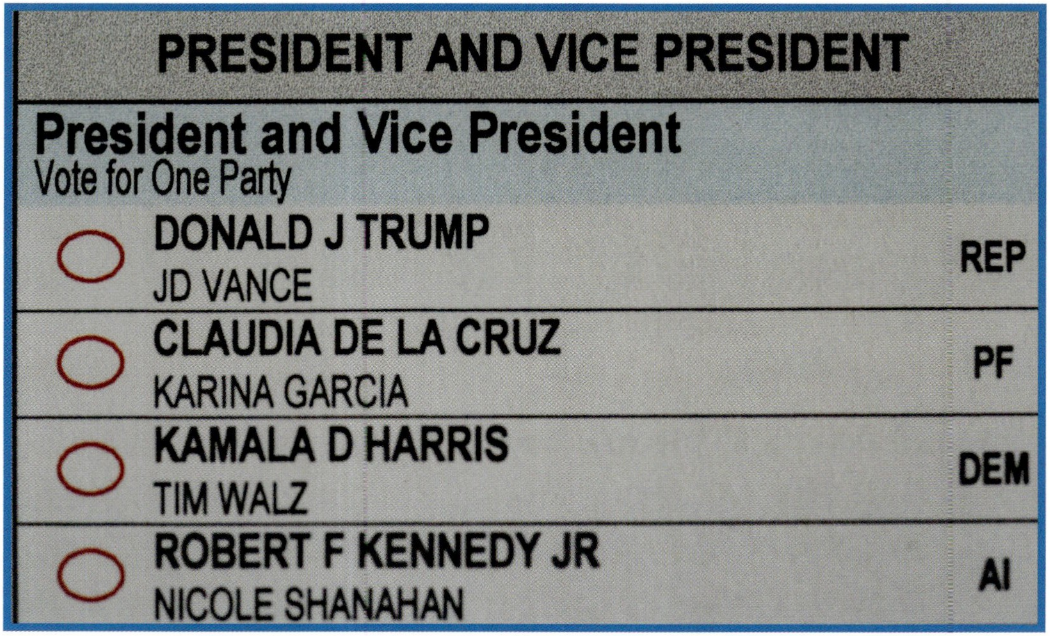

Presidents choose vice presidents who will help them win the election and run the government. They choose someone from the same **political party**. They choose someone who shares their beliefs.

Vice presidents must be at least 35 years old. They must have been born in the U.S. They must have lived in the U.S. for the past 14 years.

The vice president lives in a large house on the grounds of the U.S. Naval Observatory in Washington, D.C.

After the president, the vice president is the next person in charge of the U.S. government. If the president is sick or unable to serve, the vice president takes over for a while. If the president dies, the vice president becomes president.

The vice president attends important meetings as one of the president's top advisers. He or she is a member of the president's **cabinet**.

Vice presidents travel around the country and the world. They make speeches. They talk to people about the president's ideas.

The vice president has some special duties. He or she is president of the U.S. **Senate**. If senators are evenly split when they vote on a new law, the vice president gets to vote. The vice president breaks the tie.

The vice president also **presides** over counting states' votes in presidential elections.

UNITED STATES VICE PRESIDENTS

Eight vice presidents became president when the president died. They include Theodore Roosevelt, Harry Truman, and Lyndon Johnson.

Six vice presidents were later elected president. They include Thomas Jefferson, George H.W. Bush, and Joe Biden.

Gerald Ford became president after President Richard Nixon **resigned**.

SEAL OF THE PRESIDENT OF THE UNITED STATES

James David (J.D.) Vance was elected the 50th vice president of the United States. He ran on the **ticket** with President Donald J. Trump.

GOVERNING THE UNITED STATES

The vice president has an important job. He or she is the president's **ally** and second-in-charge.

Who is the current U.S. vice president? How do the vice president's decisions affect you?

GLOSSARY

ally (AL-eye): someone who is on your side; trusted partner

cabinet (KAB-uh-nit): a group of advisers for the head of a government; cabinet members help the president make decisions and lead parts of the U.S government

constitution (kahn-sti-TOO-shuhn): a document that sets forth the basic laws of a country and that outlines the rights of its people and the power of its government

executive (ig-ZEK-yuh-tiv): related to the part of the U.S. government that carries out laws

political party (puh-LIT-i-kuhl PAR-tee): an organization that chooses candidates to run in elections for government offices; Republicans and Democrats are U.S. political parties

presides (pri-ZIDES): acts as the authority over something; leads

resigned (ri-ZINED): gave up a job or position voluntarily; quit

running mate (RUHN-ning mate): a person who runs for public office with another candidate and who has the less important position of the two

Senate (SEN-it): one half of the U.S. Congress; a body elected to make laws that includes two senators from each U.S. state

ticket (TIK-it): a list of candidates for government office that belong to the same political party

THINKING QUESTIONS

1. Which branch of the U.S. government includes the vice president?
2. How do presidents choose vice presidents?
3. What is the vice president's job in the Senate?
4. How can the vice president become president?
5. Name a vice president who became president.

INDEX

ABOUT THE AUTHOR

Francie Dolan is a writer from Seattle, Washington. She is an American history buff who loves to learn about how her country works and how it has changed over time. She jumps at the chance to travel to Washington, D.C., and visit the capital's important buildings and monuments.